COUNSELLING
CARERS

This book is dedicated to Frank, an exhausted husband who gave his all; to Val, a dedicated supporter who continues to give her all; and to all the other Franks and Vals who travel the road together.

COUNSELLING CARERS

Supporting relatives of confused elderly people living at home

ANDREW PAPADOPOULOS

WINSLOW PRESS
Telford Road, Bicester, Oxon OX6 0TS

First published in 1990 by
Winslow Press, Telford Road, Bicester, Oxon OX6 0TS
Reprinted 1992
Copyright © Andrew Papadopoulos, 1990

Phototypeset by Gecko Limited, Bicester, Oxon
02-1154/Printed in Great Britain by Hobbs the Printers, Southampton

British Library Cataloguing in Publication Data
Papadopoulos, Andrew
Counselling carers
1. Carers of mentally disordered old persons. Counselling
I. Title
361.323

ISBN 0-86388-085-1

Contents

——Acknowledgements——

My thanks and acknowledgements go to Age Concern, Kingstanding, Hazel Murphy (social worker), various trainees from the Birmingham MSc Clinical Psychology Course, the Alzheimer's Disease Society, Birmingham, and the Departments of Psychology, Occupational Therapy and the Community Psychiatric Nursing Services based at All Saints Hospital, Birmingham who were involved in the initial development and research into carer support services.

My thanks also to Jim Dutton and Christine Adams of the Association of Chartered Physiotherapists in Psychiatry (West Midlands Branch), who have supported the development of associated training workshops.

I should like to express my gratitude to Helene Elia-Papadopoulos (speech therapist, Dudley Road Hospital) for her advice on various chapters in the book, and to various members of Solihull Health Authority and Social Services for their support in the preparation of the manuscript.

To Winslow Press for publication of the manuscript and last, but not least, to all the relatives and support workers with whom I have had the pleasure of working.

Preface

The past decade has witnessed a surge of interest in the plight of relatives who care for their elderly confused dependants. This interest has been fuelled in part by pressure from the voluntary sector, which has for many years been advocating the right of relatives to have both their contribution to their dependant's care and their own needs recognised in terms of service provision.

A second lobby has developed from the fields of adult psychiatry and learning difficulties, where research has shown the immense value of incorporating relatives into the treatment and care of their dependants.

Finally, a third avenue of support has been via recent government reports emphasising the need to develop community services to dependent people. For this objective to be realised, relatives themselves must be formally incorporated into the planning and implementation process. Arguably, therefore, they must be given formal recognition of their role, supported in their contribution to their dependant's care and provided with a range of services to support their own personal needs.

Whilst there already exists a wide body of literature for carers themselves, in terms of providing information regarding the nature and causes of confusion, financial, social, health and voluntary services available to them, and advice on management, little is available for support workers, in terms of developing their own skills in their work with relatives.

This book attempts in part to meet this gap by offering a comprehensive and thorough review of existing knowledge on the nature and causes of confusion in the elderly; an insight into the characteristics, problems and needs of relatives; psychosocial methods in the management of confused behaviour; client-centred counselling skills for helping relatives come to terms with interpersonal difficulties; and advice on setting up client-centred relative support services.

It is intended that the book should be appropriate to a wide readership but particularly to those professional and non-professional people who work with relatives and who belong to recognised agencies involved in the care of confused elderly people.

Introduction

Caring for an individual who suffers from confusion is an extremely stressful and often uncompromising task, even for those who are professionally trained in the giving of care. For relatives who are not trained and who may have strong attachment to their dependant, the experience of caring and sharing their lives with a confused person can be particularly daunting.

In addition to the difficulties relatives may encounter in providing basic day-to-day care, they also face the prolonged strain of continual demand for supervision, social disablement, lack of sleep and time for themselves, interpersonal conflicts and the grief of gradually losing the person they once knew and loved.

In the past, statutory services have tended to view confusion as a medical issue. The provision of services has therefore tended to convert confused people into patients, isolating them from society and delivering care in a passive way. Over recent years, however, professional and non-professional agencies have gradually come to realise, first, that disablement of any kind is as much a social issue as it is a health issue; second, that disabled people have the right of access to a normalised life-style; third, that services need to facilitate independent living, not make people passive recipients of care; and, finally, that the disablement affects not just the individual but their relatives, friends and indeed their close social community.

As a consequence, it is becoming widely accepted that any agency working with a confused person must also work with their relatives if holistic care is to be achieved. Practically this means recognising the needs of both dependants and relatives as a single system, respecting the contribution relatives can make towards the care of their dependants and developing a range of flexible support options which suit the system at any given point in time. Whilst each relative has their own unique needs, research in this area has shown that relatives in general require five principal areas of support:

1 A regular break from the demands of 24-hour care and supervision;

2 Practical help and guidance, both in the day-to-day management of their dependant's needs and in coping with often debilitating behaviour problems;

3 Meaningful knowledge regarding their dependant's disorder, what to expect in the future and what services are available to them;

4 A confidant(e) to talk to about the emotional consequences of caring;

5 A major say in decisions surrounding the care of their dependant.

Respite and advocacy need to be integral in the general practice of any care system; nevertheless there remains a role for caring agencies to offer the necessary support, advice and counselling to help relatives in their roles.

The following guide attempts to provide individuals wishing to develop relative support services with awareness as to the difficulties that relatives face, a basic understanding of confusion and its management, introductory counselling skills to help relatives work through their interpersonal difficulties and guidelines towards developing client-based support systems.

It is not the remit of this guide to outline specific nursing skills, medical or paramedical therapies, or to advise on current financial or legal aspects of caring. These issues require professional help and guidance and should always be sought as and when the need arises. Rather, the guide offers a full range of information and skills to help supporters to help relatives effectively.

ANDREW PAPADOPOULOS qualified as a Clinical Psychologist in 1985 from the University of Leeds and spent several years developing mental health services for the over-65s in West Birmingham Health Authority. During this time he was involved in the development of carers' support services in association with Age Concern Kingstanding and the Alzheimer's Disease Society, Birmingham Branch. He has researched into the application of psychological methods towards stress management amongst carers and has taught extensively at national level in the area of carer counselling.

Andrew currently heads the District Psychology Specialty for the over-65s in Solihull Health Authority and is honorary tutor at the School of Psychology, Birmingham University.

1
The Issues

THE NEED FOR SUPPORT

Agencies who provide care for confused people are recognising the importance of incorporating principles of 'normalisation' in the planning and delivery of services. Broadly speaking, the main theme for normalisation is that all people, irrespective of sex, race, culture, age or disability, have the right to be valued and treated as any other member of society. This means that society must first recognise the confused person as an individual in their own right with the same basic needs as any other person but one who, in addition, has other more specific needs which arise from their disablement. Second, that confused people, like most individuals, do not exist in a vacuum. They too have friends and relatives who themselves live with and are influenced by the confusion and who have much to contribute to their dependant's care. Third, that confused people and their relatives have the right to demand the types of services they feel they need and not simply to have provisions imposed according to what others seem to think they need. Each relative is different, with their own particular difficulties and their own particular needs.

It is impossible to obtain an accurate figure of those people suffering from long-term confusional states, but it is likely that approximately 6·5 per cent of the over-65s experience some form of long-term confusion, rising to approximately twenty per cent in the over-80s. The very nature of confusion often renders the individual totally incapable of looking after themselves, which means that they need substantial levels of highly-skilled care and supervision. Yet only five per cent of all elderly people are cared for in residential settings and research shows that this five per cent does not necessarily reflect the greatest dependency levels for care. The majority of confused and often totally dependent people are in fact cared for in the community by their own relatives.

Unlike professional carers, relatives are not specially trained; nor do they have the facilities to care for their confused partners. They are often frail elderly people themselves who are emotionally involved and in many cases remain with their relatives for 24 hours a day. For these people, caring is a way of life to which they are least able to adjust but, for many reasons, they wish to continue to live with and care for their confused partners. It is therefore appropriate that the caring professions address the needs of relatives in such a way as to enable and not disable them in carrying out their wishes.

Points to Remember

■Confused people need to be valued, respected and afforded the same rights as any other member of society.

■Approximately 6·5 per cent of the over-65s suffer from long-term confusion, rising to approximately twenty per cent in the over-80s.

■The majority of confused people reside in the community and are cared for by their own relatives.

■Services need to be enabling, not disabling, and to appreciate the contribution that a relative can make towards the care of their dependants.

UNDERSTANDING THE RELATIVES

Whilst a proportion of relatives are the adult children, by far the greatest part of care is done by spouses, primarily women, who are themselves elderly and very often have their own frailties to contend with.

Exactly how long a relative will continue to care for their dependant varies considerably. In cases of dementia, the literature suggests that the average duration of care is between six and eight years, although this depends upon a number of factors, including: the degree of dependency, the frequency and severity of the dependant's behaviour problems, the nature of the relationship between relative and dependant, the relative's ability to provide care and the availability of both social and practical support.

Research investigating differences between adult child's and spouse's approach to care has shown that the adult child tends to have more of a 'care manager' role; that is, they identify their relative's needs and attempt to liaise and co-ordinate with services to provide care in the best possible way. Further, given that they are likely to have other commitments themselves (family, work etc) they tend to maintain a greater emotional and practical distance than the spouse. Spouses are seen as being 'care providers'. They will identify their partner's needs, but usually meet them directly, often at great cost to themselves. Whether the relative is an adult child or a spouse, the task of caring for and sharing life with a confused person is extremely difficult.

Firstly, there is the enormous degree of stress and strain experienced as a result of simply attempting to cope with the day-to-day problems that confusion brings. Primarily these include: incontinence, nocturnal wandering, general over-demanding behaviour (eg. asking the same question over and over again) and an objection to being cared for which often results in verbal or physical aggression. In addition there is the difficulty encountered in effective communication, the constant need for supervision and the bizarre and often embarrassing behaviour which usually occurs at the most unpredictable times (eg. undressing during Sunday lunch).

At a physical level, stress is experienced as muscle tension, fatigue, regular heart palpitations and poor sleep. At an emotional level, there are difficulties in sustaining normal tolerance levels, feelings of desperation, loneliness and extreme sadness. As the problems in caring become more severe, the relative will find themselves gradually becoming withdrawn from society, their confidence in coping declines and they may regress to anger or complete withdrawal in an effort to defend themselves from total emotional and physical burn-out. Then they may experience the burden of guilt at having responded in this way or being unable to give any more of their time or effort.

Secondly, there is the progressive loss of any gratification in the relationship with the dependant. The person the relative once knew, the relationship they once shared, are now gone and they are left with an incomplete shell — a shattered world with few if any passing moments of the life they once had.

The experience of prolonged grief is perhaps the most difficult issue that a relative has to endure. Coping with and growing through grief requires time, space and expression. All too often, the relative is simply unable to work through their grief because caring in itself requires all their efforts. It is not surprising, therefore, that a relative's primary need is relief from constant supervision ('respite care'). This may include regular day care, occasional 24-hour limited care and/or 24-hour care for holiday periods. Given that relatives are not professionally trained in either providing day-to-day care or in the management of problem behaviour, they do require some form of support and training in respect of these two areas. In order to manage confusion, relatives need to have a proper understanding of their relative's disorder. All too often relatives have limited, if any, knowledge about the nature and causes of confusion. If they do have some knowledge this is likely to reflect the more medical aspects of confusion, which in itself does not provide an objective basis from which to develop management skills or to adjust emotionally to the difficulties that confusion brings. Finally, there are the immense emotionally-based problems that a relative may face, which very often require skilled support and counselling, particularly with those difficulties relating to guilt and negative self-worth, bereavement, stress and family discord.

Points to Remember

■Carers are in the main spouses, primarily women, who are themselves elderly and frail.

■The approximate duration of caring for a confused relative is between six and eight years.

■Carers can be divided into care managers and care providers.

■The problems which cause the greatest degree of stress and strain are those related to incontinence, nocturnal wandering, general over-demanding behaviour and an objection to being cared for.

■The needs of relatives relate to respite care, support and training with day-to-day problem behaviour, an understanding of their dependant's disorder and someone to talk to, formally or informally, regarding their interpersonal difficulties.

THE ROLE OF THE SUPPORT WORKER

Supporting a relative through their difficulties is to a greater or lesser extent a function of anyone who is in contact with that person, from the milkman to the general practitioner. Yet not everyone is in a position to address a relative's needs consistently or objectively.

For those relatives who are in contact with statutory or non-statutory bodies, they may already have access to information, respite and support facilities. However, more often than not, the primary responsibility for such agencies is for their confused clients/patients. Consequently, if and when conflicts arise between the relative and the agency's client, the agency involved must ultimately support the needs of their client, which may compromise any existing relationship that the agency may have with the client's relatives.

Notwithstanding the needs of the clients, relatives themselves need access to a support system which is accountable solely to themselves, a system which considers the relative as a separate unit/client, enjoying the same degree of confidentiality as is given to their dependants. The 'support worker' is seen as such a system, whose role is to provide objective, confidential and structured support to the relative. In particular, the support worker should have a reasonably clear understanding of the difficulties that relatives face, knowledge regarding the nature and causes of confusion, basic skills in the management of confused behaviour and a range of counselling skills to help relatives work through their own particular emotionally-based difficulties. Whilst the support worker may be able to offer additional skills related to their own professional backgrounds, they are not offering a service in their professional capacity: a support worker should be seen as a separate entity, not directly involved with the confused person. In addition, although the support worker must at all times observe the confidentiality of their client, in those circumstances where there is some form of link with other involved parties it is proper that the support worker inform those agencies (eg. general practitioner, social worker, nurse) that they are involved with the patient/client's relatives.

Finally, supporting and counselling relatives in difficulty is in itself stressful. It is therefore strongly advisable that the support worker obtains appropriate supervision prior to working with a client.

Points to Remember

■Relatives themselves need access to personal support and counselling in addition to what may be offered for their dependants.

■The support worker is seen as such a facility, providing confidential and structured support, meaningful information and advice on the day-to-day management of confusion-related difficulties.

■The support worker should always advise other agencies involved in the care of the confused person that they are working with the relatives.

■The support worker themselves should always obtain back-up support prior to working with relatives.

2
Confusion and its Management

THE NATURE AND CAUSES OF CONFUSION

Confusion can be defined as an altered state of perception, awareness and memory which gives rise to behaviour which, to the observer, seems incompatible both with reality and with the demands of the environment. To the confused individual, it is the experience of a fragmented and disorganised world over which they have little, if any, control. Aggression, prolonged fear, wandering or complete withdrawal are often common responses that a confused person will make in an effort to adapt to that world.

Before attempting to understand confusion, it is important to provide at least a simple outline of the normal functioning of the brain. The human brain is the 'conductor of the orchestra', in that it coordinates all aspects of bodily function in perfect harmony. It is also the central mechanism of the body which gives us conscious experience of the world around us. It allows us to make sense of our experiences, to think in very complex ways and to feel a variety of emotions.

Like a computer, the brain has both a hardware and a software component. The hardware is the billions of nerve cells which make up the structure of the brain and the vast network of blood vessels which feed the brain with oxygen and foodstuffs in order that it can live and function effectively. The software is the brain's internal 'programme', the set of rules which govern the way brain cells communicate with each other. The programme dictates from birth what parts of the brain will have which particular functions. How these parts operate in terms of our individual ways of thinking and feeling is shaped by our experiences as we grow throughout life.

Broadly speaking, the posterior regions of the brain (parietal and occipital lobes) are necessary for sensation, vision and perception. The middle or temporal regions are necessary for speech, language, emotions and the memory of recent experiences. The frontal regions have a variety of functions, but are particularly important in the co-ordination of complex movement, problem-solving and the control of the emotional aspects of our personality. Finally, the inner, more central parts of the brain have a particular role in co-ordinating basic bodily functions and contain the nerve fibres which carry messages to and from the outer parts of the brain (cortex) to the rest of the body.

The brain is built to withstand and adapt to changes caused, for example, by minor damage or toxins. However, if these changes are either prolonged or too severe in that they may upset the balance in a major way, then confusion often ensues. The younger the brain, the more easily it is able to redress this balance. As the brain grows older it becomes more sensitive to changes and is less able to compensate for them. Such changes can either be reversible, in that they last for relatively short periods of time and can be alleviated with proper medical care, or irreversible, in that they cause major/progressive damage to the hardware and ultimately to the software of the brain itself.

Reversible changes that give rise to 'acute' or short-lived confusional states are often caused by toxins (by-products of infections) which temporarily upset the brain's natural chemistry. In the elderly, such 'toxic confusional states' are common with disorders of the urinal–genital system (kidney failure, urinary tract infection etc), respiratory system (bronchitis), food poisoning or even a severe influenza virus. Other causes are lack of certain vitamins and minerals in the diet (especially vitamin B-complex and iron), disorders of the hormonal system (eg. diabetes and hypothyroidism), or periodically poor blood supply to the brain due to diseases of the heart and blood vessels.

Sometimes acute confusional states can also occur following the onset of a psychiatric illness, such as major depression, stressful life events or even some form of late-life psychotic disturbance. If a relative reports that their dependant has 'all of a sudden' become confused or has begun to show very bizarre behaviour, it is always advisable to suggest that they seek medical attention first. The majority of the causes for acute confusional states are curable or at least manageable with proper medical care.

Irreversible changes that give rise to long-term and increasing confusion are in the main due to progressive (chronic) brain damage, particularly to those outer parts of the brain which are associated with intellectual functioning and personality. The term 'dementia' is often given to such conditions and affects approximately six per cent of the over-65s, rising to approximately twenty per cent in the over-80s. A tiny proportion of younger people suffer with certain forms of dementia, but the condition is mainly found in late life.

Within this age group, there are two main forms of dementia: Alzheimer's Disease and what is known medically as multi-infarct or arterio-sclerotic dementia. Whilst both forms are progressive and give rise to long-term confusion, their presentation, causes and implications for the relative are somewhat different.

Multi-infarct Dementia

The term literally means multiple blockages in the small blood vessels of the brain. The condition occurs because the blood vessels become clogged up with fatty material, rather like a lead pipe which becomes clogged up with mineral deposits, which restricts the supply of water through the pipe. Eventually a small deposit of fatty material can break away and find its way to the brain, becoming lodged at the entrance to a tiny blood vessel, thereby cutting off the blood supply to the surrounding brain tissue. Within the space of a few minutes the surrounding tissue dies and its functions are lost.

When an individual suffers such an injury the onset of confusion is quite marked. For example, they may be out shopping and suddenly wander off, to be found some time afterwards in a very disorientated state. This initial confusion is likely to last for approximately two to three weeks, until the major biological effects of the injury have resolved (eg. reabsorption of surrounding fluid). What is left, in terms of the individual's behaviour and intellectual disablement, is likely to be permanent, although this depends upon the extent and sites of damaged nerve cells.

The major difficulty in managing this type of dementia is that it is extremely unpredictable. A person may suffer a series of infarcts over a short period of time, then be more or less spared a further injury for the rest of their lives. This means that the condition is not necessarily fatal in itself, although the usual course of this disorder is a succession of strokes until the brain is no longer able to sustain itself or the body and death eventually occurs.

There is no evidence to date that the condition is inherited. Rather, high blood pressure, prolonged stress, heavy smoking, a fatty diet and diabetes are all closely associated as causal factors. Whilst there is no cure, in that when brain damage is sustained it is irreversible, there are circumstances where intensive rehabilitation (eg. memory retraining, activity training, speech therapy), if available, can help the individual to compensate for their disabilities.

Diagnosis of multi-infarct dementia is based upon: a history of acute confusional states; the absence of any evidence to suggest other reversible causes for the confusion; the possible presence of associated factors, such as high blood pressure; evidence from brain scan investigations which show one or more areas of low density in the brain; and neuropsychological assessment which would show localised/focused brain impairment.

Alzheimer's Disease

Alzheimer's Disease, or 'senile dementia of the Alzheimer's type', is a disorder of the brain tissue itself where vast numbers of nerve cells begin to degenerate fairly rapidly throughout the cortex. Initially, personality and intellectual functioning are affected, although as the degeneration spreads it begins to affect those internal structures of the brain that deal with basic bodily functions. Unlike multi-infarct dementia, Alzheimer's Disease is in itself fatal, even though other diseases (eg. pneumonia) are likely to cause mortality towards the latter stages of the condition.

To date there is no reliable evidence to suggest a possible cause or trigger for the condition, though there does seem to be strong evidence for a genetic (family) link, in that certain individuals are, from birth, at risk of developing Alzheimer's Disease in later life. However the actual probability of a relative developing Alzheimer's Disease, even though they may be at risk, is very small.

Diagnosis of Alzheimer's Disease is made on the basis of: a history of progressive and gradual memory loss; generally poor performance on psychological tests; the results of brain scan investigations which would show generalised brain shrinkage (cortical atrophy) with an associated enlargement of the fluid-filled spaces of the brain (ventricular enlargement). However some professionals would argue that even these measures together are not totally reliable in effecting a diagnosis which, ultimately, can only be made on autopsy.

In any event, diagnosing Alzheimer's Disease is notoriously difficult in the early stages of the disorder and, in consequence, it is impossible to state precisely how long a person may be likely to suffer the disease, although estimates suggest around eight to twelve years. Ironically, the younger the individual the faster and more aggressive is the dementia.

In terms of its presentation, the initial symptom of Alzheimer's Disease is global forgetfulness of recent actions or experiences. This is because those parts of the brain which are responsible for transferring our immediate experiences into long-term memory become dysfunctional. This does not, however, prevent experiences already stored in the long-term memory from being retrieved. Thus a person may forget that they have had a visitor moments earlier, but can nevertheless remember with great accuracy a holiday they had several years previously. Eventually, even long-term memory becomes patchy and broken, to the point where the sufferer can no longer recognise their home or their family as they are, but can only identify them from earlier photographs — if at all. At this time, personality becomes fragmented and disinhibited. The individual may behave as though they have no conception of where they are or who they are with. They may respond irrationally to simple instructions or exhibit flights of delusional ideas.

Communication difficulties are also evident. Often the sufferer will be unable to find the right word for familiar objects or speak in total jargon (aphasia). They will be unable to carry out simple sequences of movement (motor apraxia): for example, they might put their clothes on in the wrong order, be unable to make a cup of tea or even solve simple problems or comprehend simple instructions, and will most likely be disorientated in terms of time, place and person.

In the latter stages, even feeding themselves can become a problem. Disinhibition of behaviour develops into a disinhibition of bodily functions including incontinence and they may be unlikely to interpret accurately sensations such as pain (sensory agnosia). Perhaps the most difficult change of all for both the relative and the sufferer to endure is the overall indignity which surrounds this devastating disorder.

Points to Remember

■Confused behaviour is the product of an altered state of perception, awareness and memory.

■To the confused, confusion is the experience of a fragmented and disorganised world.

■Confusion is caused by a disruption to either the hardware or the software of the brain.

■The two main disorders which give rise to confusion (as a result of brain damage) in the over-65s are Alzheimer's Disease and multi-infarct dementia.

■Multi-infarct dementia is characterised by a history of acute confusional states and step-wise deterioration in intellectual and personality functioning. It is usually, but not always in itself, a fatal condition.

■Alzheimer's Disease is characterised by a slow, insidious onset of memory loss, followed by disintegration of the personality and eventual disinhibition of bodily functions. It is a fatal condition and has a genetic basis.

MANAGING CONFUSED BEHAVIOUR — BASIC PRINCIPLES

Managing the often frequent occurrence of confused behaviour not only relies on the relatives' understanding of brain–behaviour relationships and other aspects that influence behaviour, but also on the degree to which they are able to readdress their own behavioural and emotional boundaries which may have existed with their partner prior to their illness.

In addition, therefore, to helping the relative achieve an understanding, it is also important that the support worker addresses the client's difficulties in coming to terms with these boundary changes. From sharing life as a partner/adult child, the relative progressively becomes more of a carer and their confused partner a dependant. For example, such issues as bathing require major behavioural and emotional adaptations from the relative.

Simply stated, behaviour is the product of a series of stages which help us to adapt to both our internal (bodily) and external environment. We obtain information through our senses (eyes, ears, nose etc) which is then temporarily stored and coded by the brain (perception) in such a form as to make this information accessible to meaningful interpretation (comprehension). Once this information is in a meaningful form, the brain consciously or unconsciously makes a decision as to whether or not we need to act upon it. If the conclusion is to act, then the brain sets in motion a series of output signals to the rest of the body, which give rise to behaviour. If one's behaviour is successful and achieves its goal, in that there is some pay-off (reinforcement), then the chances that the behaviour will take place again in similar situations are increased. If, however, the behaviour fails to achieve positive pay-off, or the consequences are in some way negative, then the behaviour is unlikely to occur again (see Figure 2.1).

Whilst the consequences of our behaviour determine the extent to which we are likely to repeat it under similar circumstances, the precise nature of the behaviour is influenced by many other factors. These include: the way we feel at the time; our attitudes and beliefs about ourselves in the situation; our ability to solve problems and to make appropriate decisions; whether or not we have observed others behaving in similar circumstances in the past; and our previous experiences. In this way we learn to adapt and cope with the demands that are made upon us in our everyday lives.

Crucial to the way in which we make sense of our world, and to the way in which we learn to cope with it, is our ability to store and recall information when needed. Without a memory we cannot func-

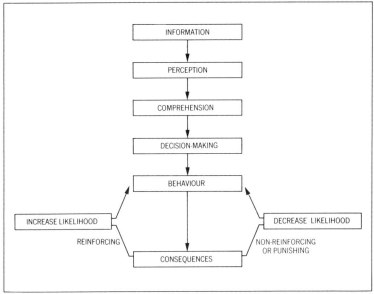

Figure 2.1 **The behavioural process**

tion. Indeed the extent to which we are orientated to time, place and person relies extensively on the ability to remember recent events (short-term memory). If these recent events are particularly meaningful or important, we are able to transfer these experiences into long-term memory, to be recalled as and when needed.

By way of an example, one can imagine a postman delivering mail to a house. He approaches the house, walks through the gate and gets ready to post the mail as he has done many times before. All of a sudden, the postman is confronted by a large dog. The postman's brain processes this information and concludes that the dog is in fact a threat to him. The brain then makes the body aware of this threat by increasing the postman's arousal levels. If the postman feels he is unlikely to cope with the threat (because of past experiences, possibly poor self-confidence, a 'more than his job's worth' attitude towards his work etc) then he is likely to make a hasty retreat from the house.

The consequences of his exit bring relief (reinforcement) in that the dog is no longer a threat. As a result, the postman is more likely to avoid the house during future deliveries or to negotiate an alternative means of delivering the mail without confronting the dog.

Alternatively, the postman may confront the dog (because he has learned to control dogs in the past) and pacify it. Again, the consequences are relief, but this time at coping and not avoiding the situation. He will then be more likely to engage in this coping behaviour on subsequent occasions.

In summary, we can liken the learning process to a computer. Information is fed into the computer from a keyboard (senses). It is then processed in a meaningful form, so that the computer can act upon this information (perception and comprehension). The computer program (previous experiences, attitudes and belief, etc) further processes this information and arrives at a conclusion (decision-making). The conclusion is then passed to an output system, such as printer or screen (parts of the body), which displays that conclusion to the operator (observable behaviour).

If the operator is happy with the output, they may use the programme again to process similar information. If not, they will have to make adjustments to the programme — unless of course the problem is with the hardware itself, in which case the programme will also be affected.

In confused individuals, both the hardware and the software are affected. Information from the environment enters the brain normally and (apart from the more severe cases of chronic brain failure) is perceived normally, but the brain cannot process this information in a meaningful way.

Their response is therefore the product of what they construe to be reality. If, for example, their recall starts from 20 years previously, then family, friends and so on might seem totally unfamiliar. As far as they are concerned they may still think they are at work, when in fact they may be attending a day centre. Understandably, they may seem frightened or even angry. Their behaviour is simply their way of responding to a world that does not make sense.

Another function of the brain is to control our feelings and actions. This is mediated by the frontal part of the brain. When these centres are damaged, the individual and their relative are faced with the additional problem of 'disinhibition', that is the inability to control one's behaviour. Thus, even if the confused person felt that they needed to control themselves, they would be unable to do so.

Understanding those factors which influence behaviour enables us to make predictions as to occurrence and highlights a number of functions which can be manipulated to control or manage it. Behaviour is situational-specific: that is, the environment defines and triggers the onset of previously learned behaviour. For example, we are unlikely to get up and dance in the middle of a serious church sermon, unless of course we completely misunderstand the situation. Rather, we will display 'listening behaviour'.

Similarly, if a motor car driver approaches a red light he will automatically produce a sequence of movements in order to bring the vehicle to a halt. Here the red light *triggers* a previously learned sequence of behaviour. The driver behaves in this way in the presence of the red light because, in the

past, the *consequences* of stopping have been reinforcing. Over a series of such experiences, the red
light becomes associated with the behaviour by the
presence of the reinforcing consequence. One can
therefore predict that in the presence of the red light
the driver will stop.

Simply stated, this is the ABC of behaviour: A =
antecedents/triggers, B = behaviour, C = consequences. If we have an understanding of both the
triggers and the likely consequences then, using this
model, we can predict the behaviour.

Example

Mrs J reports that, each time she tries to help her
confused husband get dressed, he becomes either
verbally or physically aggressive and they both end
up in tears.

Procedure

In order to help Mrs J address her husband's difficulties effectively we must first build a workable model
that helps us clarify and predict what is happening.
This can be developed by asking a number of questions:

1 When (in what circumstances) and how often does
the aggression occur?

2 What triggers the aggression (how does Mrs J
attempt to dress her husband — what precisely
does she do)?

3 What are the consequences of her husband's
aggression (what happens afterwards which may
be reinforcing the behaviour)?

In order to obtain this information, it might be
useful to ask the client to keep a daily diary of their

ABC. Once this information is obtained, it could read as follows:

1 'Usually in the morning, hardly at all at night time.'

2 'I wake him up, then tell him to take off his pyjamas in the nicest possible way, at which point he will get angry and hit out at me.'

3 'I cannot help but get angry back. I might also hit him, depending on how I feel. We can both have a real boxing match.'

Analysis

Antecedent/trigger = 'Take off your pyjamas, dear.'
Behaviour = aggression.
Consequence = aggression/retaliation.

Conclusions

Given that Mr J is suffering from dementia, it is likely that he is much more confused in the morning than at any other time in the day. After all, during the day he is active and is therefore more likely to be aware of his surroundings. Mr J also suffers from exceptionally poor memory and simply does not recognise Mrs J as being his wife. As far as he is concerned, he wakes up to find a strange lady asking him to take his clothes off. If, previous to his dementia, Mr J was an independent and modest gentleman, then understandably he will respond in this way. In addition, given also that Mr J might be unable to control his emotion, it is likely that he will over-compensate.

Mrs J finds it very difficult to accept the severity of her husband's problems. Like her husband, she too is an independent person and has never really had any experience of caring for adults in this way. She has brought up children, but Mr J is her husband, not a child, and she does not want to treat him like one. As a result, she takes her husband's anger personally, feels hurt and retaliates as a way of defending herself against this hurt. Unfortunately, the retaliation is itself a strong 'reinforcing element', which increases the likelihood of his displaying further aggression. The more she retaliates, the more she reinforces his anger.

Solutions

■In the first place, Mrs J needs to have an objective understanding of her husband's difficulties and why he behaves in this way.

■She will require support and counselling in coming to terms with the loss of the relationship she once knew and in having more of a caring role.

■In terms of effecting control over her husband's behaviour, there are two lines of attack she may wish to try: (a) change the triggers; (b) change the consequences.

The triggers. Given that Mr J is very confused in the morning, she might attempt to wake him up gradually and help him to *orientate* himself by 'cueing him in' to the fact that it is morning (eg. "What a lovely morning, Jack. It's eight o'clock, you must be hungry, breakfast will soon be ready").

Following on, she might first present Mr J with his day clothes before taking off his pyjamas, so that he knows that the intention is to get dressed, not to have his pyjamas removed. Both these approaches help to make the situation conducive to getting dressed.

Mrs J might also use *reminiscence* cues as a way of helping her husband understand why he should put his day clothes on (eg. "Do you remember putting on your new suit the day you went for your interview?"). *Validating* his feelings is another approach that could be used. Here, Mrs J would address her husband's feelings directly: "You seem angry, Jack; is it because you feel embarrassed?" Finally, the use of *distraction* might help to shift Mr J's attention from what Mrs J is doing. Distraction methods can be very useful, but Mrs J needs to know or experiment with the things which are likely to distract her husband's attention sufficiently from the task in hand. For example, such methods may include: discussion as to the weather or recent events in the news; giving him an old photograph of the family to look at; asking him if he can remember when the photograph was taken, and so on.

The consequences. As a general rule, if the reinforcer is removed the behaviour is far more likely to stop. Technically, this is known as 'time-out': that is, time-out from positive reinforcement. In this case, Mrs J's confrontation is seen to be the reinforcer. If, therefore, her husband starts to become aggressive she can try removing the reinforcer by not retaliating and getting on with the task in hand.

Perhaps more appropriately, she could simply remove herself from the room until they have both had a chance to calm down. After all, her husband's aggression is also likely to be reinforcing her own retaliations. If, even as a result of changing the triggers or removing the reinforcer, Mr J begins to allow his wife to dress him, it is important that she reinforces this appropriate behaviour by praising him at each step in the process.

While the above procedure, if carried out consistently, is likely to prove very effective, it is not fail-safe in all circumstances. Sometimes the confused person may be excessively anxious or be responding to delusional ideas or hallucinations. If behavioural management alone is unhelpful, then the matter should be discussed with the dependant's general practitioner who might consider it appropriate to provide additional help in the form of medication.

Finally, the primary objective of counselling is to help the client find their own solution once they are able to fully understand the rationale behind the procedure. It is important, therefore, to encourage the client to come up with their own ideas but, ideally, these solutions should be based upon the principles outlined above.

Points to Remember

■Relatives need to understand their dependant's behaviour in order to manage it.

■Relatives will require a degree of support in coming to terms with their changing role.

■Behaviour is adaptive and is the product of a process involving reception, perception, comprehension and decision-making.

■If behaviour is reinforced, it is likely to occur again under similar circumstances.

■If behaviour is not reinforced, or if the consequences are in some way negative, the behaviour is unlikely to recur in similar situations.

■The precise nature of behaviour is influenced by attitudes and beliefs, the situational triggers, problem-solving ability, previous learning experiences and biological make-up.

■Memory is crucial to the way in which we make sense of our experiences and in our ability to orientate ourselves to our current circumstances.

■Confused people fail to derive appropriate meaning from their experiences largely as a result of impaired cognitive processing.

■Confused individuals may also experience difficulties in controlling their behaviour because of a destruction of nerve pathways necessary to initiate control.

■Behaviour is situational-specific, in that the situation/environment defines and triggers behavioural sequences.

■Predicting behaviour is based upon the ABC model, where
A = triggers/antecedents,
B = behaviour and
C = consequences (reinforcing, non-reinforcing or punishing).

■Managing problem behaviour is primarily based upon manipulation of either the antecedents, the consequences or both. Manipulating the triggers involves the use of orientation, validation, distraction and manipulation of the physical environment in order that it becomes conducive to triggering appropriate behaviour.
  Manipulation of the consequences involves the use of 'time-out' to decrease the frequency of inappropriate behaviour and reinforcement to increase the occurrence of appropriate behaviour.

■Behavioural methods can often be supplemented by medical intervention and the advice of the client's medical officer should always be sought when necessary.

MANAGING CONFUSED BEHAVIOUR
— COMMON PROBLEMS

The use of the principles outlined in the preceding section may serve to manage the following and often frequent difficulties.

Communication Difficulties

The first step is to ensure that the relative's dependant is not suffering from any sensory deficits, such as eyesight or hearing difficulties.

Very often the confused individual may be unable to make proper sense out of verbal instructions. It is important to encourage the relative to use as many different forms of non-verbal communication as possible (eg. written instructions, clear pictures, miming/gestures). Where verbal communication is possible although limited, it might help to keep instructions simple but to the point.

Changing the way in which a relative communicates with their dependant takes time and repeated effort and therefore they are likely to require a great deal of support in carrying this out effectively.

Memory Difficulties

The confused person is likely to experience difficulties not only with respect to short-term memory but also in being able to remember how to accomplish certain tasks, such as dressing or making a cup of tea.

Two main lines of intervention may be helpful here. First, the use of clear instructions, reminders, calendars, clocks and so on placed in strategic positions around the home may help both to orientate and remind the dependant as to the time of day, recent and future events or how they are to accomplish certain tasks. In addition, it is likely that they will be unable to use certain items of modern equipment, owing to relearning difficulties. However they may be able to use older equipment quite adequately. Where it is safe to do so, it may be useful to advise the relatives to make available certain items which their dependant was able to use in the past (eg. whistling kettles, lever-operated tin-openers).

Second, the relative could attempt to remind their dependant as to how they used to accomplish certain tasks in the past. If this approach is attempted, it is important to take each task slowly and in small stages, and to praise their dependant if they are successful in accomplishing each stage.

Wandering

Wandering is a common problem, especially in severely confused individuals. It occurs for a variety of reasons and, like any other form of behaviour, it is usually purposeful. People may wander because they may feel frightened at finding themselves in unfamiliar circumstances and thus seek a person or place offering security. Or they may be responding to a thought or idea that they may have at the time; for example, they may believe that they are still at work and may therefore leave the breakfast table, put on their coat and attempt to travel to work as they would have done in the past. Wandering may also be triggered by some biological drive, such as a need to go to the toilet, or they may be hungry. They are not entirely sure where to go in order to satisfy their need.

Again, the use of simple messages left at strategic points around the home, informing the dependant where their relative may be, how to get to the lavatory, what time of day it is and so on may prove useful. Leaving a light on in the bedroom at night might also help the dependant reorientate themselves should they wake up in the night and feel frightened.

If the dependant is likely to wander off outside the home, then it is advisable that the relative makes sure that the dependant has a clear and accessible form of identity about their person. Restricting access to certain rooms, especially restricting access to the front door by the use of unobtrusive locks or difficult-to-open door handles and so on could be tried, although this can often lead to agitation in the confused person.

If the dependant needs to be restrained in some way during a wandering episode, the relative should try to stay as calm as possible and use gentle physical prompting as a way of reassuring their dependant. Finally, distraction methods may also prove to be very useful at such times.

Aggression

Aggression, whether it occurs frequently or infrequently, is often particularly distressing, both to the dependant and relative, and may cause additional problems with other family members, especially children.

It is important that the relative has a clear understanding as to why the aggression is taking place and, if possible, is able to predict its occurrence (the ABC model). The procedure outlined in the case example in the previous section should always be attempted. However, should this prove to be ineffective, it is advisable to seek the advice of the client's general practitioner or medical officer, who may be able to offer medical assistance where this is felt to be appropriate.

Over-demanding Behaviour

Persistent questioning and a constant desire by the dependant to seek their relative's reassuring presence are perhaps the most frequent and the most stressful problems to have to cope with. At times, gentle reassurance may be all that is needed, especially in the mildly confused individual. However, in more severe cases, it may be necessary to use written or illustrated instructions as to where the relative may be or what their dependant should be doing. Distraction methods may prove helpful, although it is unlikely that the dependant will be able to sustain their attention on a task for any reasonable length of time.

Perhaps the most beneficial approach, if available, is to seek and develop some form of regular respite. This may involve having someone else come into the home for short periods of time to supervise the dependant, thereby affording the relative an opportunity to have time for themselves or to seek some form of daily respite, such as day centre or day hospital care, access to which will need to be via social services or the client's general practitioner.

Personal Hygiene

In circumstances where the relative may find extreme difficulty in being able to address personal hygiene issues with their dependants, it may be advisable to contact social services, who may be able to offer some assistance.

Incontinence

Incontinence is a common feature in severe cases of dementia. It occurs primarily because the mechanisms in the brain which serve to inhibit the bladder and bowels from opening involuntarily are damaged. Under normal circumstances, when the bladder or bowels are full, the message is sent to the brain and the brain in turn assesses whether or not it may be appropriate to let the bladder and bowels release the contents. The actual release mechanism itself is accomplished via a reflex arc in the spine. In dementia, however, whilst the nerve pathways that take information to the brain from the bladder and bowels and the reflex arc at the base of the spine are intact, the brain itself cannot send inhibitory impulses to the bladder or bowels because the central mechanisms in the brain that are responsible for carrying out this action are impaired. As a result, the individual will feel the desire to go to the toilet, and will indeed make moves in that direction, but will be unable to hold themselves until they reach it. The consequences of incontinence are as embarrassing to the dependant as they are to the relative.

If incontinence is a difficulty, it is always advisable to seek medical attention first, since many forms of incontinence may be the result of some factor other than brain failure. If it is clear that the incontinence is symptomatic of a dementing illness, then the following suggestions may help:

■Regular toileting. It may be possible to predict the likelihood of the dependant wishing to go to the toilet and thereby to build toileting into the daily routine.

■Making access to the toilet easy. This may involve the use of a commode close to the dependant's bed, providing clear directional signs towards the toilet, and making undressing a relatively easy process, for example by replacing buttons or zips with Velcro fasteners.

■Protection. Given that accidents are likely to occur, it may be helpful to protect items of bedding and furniture by covering them with some form of unobtrusive but waterproof material, such as a plastic sheet underneath the ordinary sheet or waterproof upholstery covers. In addition, incontinence pads are available and may be considered as a way of preventing the indignity that an individual may suffer, especially when in the presence of others.

Again, social services may also be able to advise as to whether or not an incontinence laundry service exists in the locality. Some hospitals also provide a continence advisory service, so it is always worthwhile making enquiries.

On a final note, the management of specific difficulties may require professional help and advice. Where this is needed, it is advisable that the relative seeks the involvement of their local community psychiatric nurse as a first step. They may be able to help directly, in terms of offering advice on the variety of management issues, and in addition may be able to facilitate contacts with other professional bodies in the health or social services. Access to community psychiatric nursing services is usually gained via the client's general practitioner.

Of particular relevance are speech therapists, occupational therapists and clinical psychologists, who are able to offer expert advice on specific behaviour problems for relatives (*see Appendix II*).

COPING IN A CRISIS

Crisis situations can be frequent and varied. As a general rule, the 'three Ps' are a useful basis for crisis management: Prediction, Preparation and Prevention.

Prediction

It may be possible to predict the likely occurrence of certain types of crises; for example, Mrs B (a confused individual) has always been responsible for preparing the evening meal, but, owing to her confusion, she is now unable to make even simple meals in the kitchen and will often prove to be very unsafe when attempting to use certain types of equipment.

Experience has shown Mr B that, if he is attempting to make the evening meal in the presence of Mrs B, she will intervene and become quite assertive in preventing him from carrying out his task. A crisis could ensue, in terms of possible aggression between the parties or with respect to the safety of both of them.

Preparation

Given that crises can occur, however well the relative may predict and therefore seek to prevent them, it is important that they have a set of contingencies which they can operate at a moment's notice, given that they are also likely to be in a stressful situation themselves and therefore unable to think clearly.

A useful method is to have a list of instructions clearly displayed in a prominent place, for example by the telephone, which clearly outlines the relevant parties that need to be contacted, what should be done in the way of controlling the crisis and what other action may be necessary to be taken after the crisis is resolved, such as contacting a named person for support.

Prevention

If one is able to predict the circumstances which could give rise to a crisis, then it may be possible to prevent the crisis from occurring by using a number of methods. For example, in the above case, Mr B might be able to prepare the evening meal the night before, once Mrs B is asleep. Alternatively, he may be able to enlist some form of help to prepare the evening meal while he takes Mrs B out shopping.

Mr B may wish to organise the preparation of the meal in such a way that Mrs B has limited and safe involvement in the process; for example, he may leave Mrs B to peel the potatoes while he puts the pans on the cooker to boil.

3
Approaches to Counselling

BASIC PRINCIPLES AND CORE SKILLS

Counselling, as an approach towards helping people work through their difficulties, assumes that individuals have the capacity within themselves to change. Counselling therefore attempts to encourage this capacity through self-awareness, exploration of feelings and confrontation of major issues, all leading to action.

Counselling methods are promoted in an atmosphere conveying trust, empathy and unconditional acceptance. Whatever the client's difficulties, whatever they are feeling or whatever they may have done, they need to be valued and accepted unconditionally. Without these aspects being present within a counselling relationship there is little room for growth.

The skills involved in counselling are developed through experience. However the way in which a counsellor interprets their client's difficulties depends to a large extent on the counsellor's understanding of human behaviour. The theoretical basis for most counselling approaches stems from a broad range of theories of human functioning, known generally as 'humanistic theory'.

While it is advisable that the reader makes further enquiry into these areas, a few central assumptions can be summarised as follows:

■Human behaviour is motivated by a number of drives directed ultimately towards self-fulfilment (self-actualising tendency).

■We are all born with the need and the ability to express our feelings openly. The various demands or experiences which we undergo as we develop through life sometimes necessitate that we suppress our feelings and desires to a degree which may give rise to psychological and biological problems that find expression in everyday life.

■We have a need to be accepted and valued by others in order that we can sustain emotional well-being. If our needs cannot be met by existing relationships or circumstances, then we tend to redirect our energy in other ways (eg. by becoming a workaholic) where some of our needs can be met, albeit indirectly. A tendency to behave in this way is termed 'displacement'.

■People have the capacity for self-preservation. Whilst displacement can be seen as one method for preventing us from emotionally 'drying out', defence mechanisms ensure that the vulnerable 'child' within us (our emotional self) is not damaged. Aggression, denial and avoidance of confrontation are all primary defence mechanisms.

Before embarking upon a decision to help anyone with their difficulties it is always worth while exploring the motivations for wanting to do so first. Helping people overcome difficulties can be immensely satisfying, but remember that you are doing it for them and not for your own personal gain. Pure self-interest can destroy therapeutic boundaries and can lead to irreparable damage to both the client and the support worker.

Be honest and open with your thoughts and feelings at all times and never hesitate to make this clear to your client. In particular, if you find yourself with thoughts and feelings towards your client which are likely to bias the relationship in any way, do obtain some form of supervision — but discuss this with your client first. Always preserve the values and dignity of the client; never break confidences unless you have their prior permission: to do otherwise can, justifiably, lead to distrust.

Finally, there may be occasions when your clients become distressed or even angry in the course of the session. It is important that you do not try to 'rescue' them from their feelings. Confronting and exploring feelings is a vital part of growing. Rather, accept and share with your client their distress.

Methods of Counselling

Attending and listening

The way in which a counsellor communicates that they are listening and attending to what their client is saying is in itself a powerful means of helping a client to express themselves. Frequent eye contact, a relaxed but upright posture, occasional nodding of the head and interjecting verbally with the odd "Mm" or "Yes, I think I understand that", are ways which convey attention. In addition, summarising what the client has said at times in the course of the session is often useful.

Open versus closed questioning

Helping the clients expand on certain themes may be achieved either by asking them a specific, focused question (eg. "Do you feel angry at what has happened to your husband?") or by asking them a more general question (eg. "How do you feel about your marriage?").

The use of direct questioning enables the counsellor to direct their clients towards important issues. Often the client will be unable to direct themselves towards certain matters because they may be too embarrassed or find it too painful to achieve this on their own.

Reflection

The term literally means rebounding what the client has said in order to help them explore the issues in hand:

Client "I want to hit her at times."
Counsellor "You want to hit her."
Client "I just get so angry and frustrated that I feel like knocking some sense into her."

In this instance, reflection has helped the client explore his feelings towards the relative. Further reflection can enable the client to expand on their feelings:

Counsellor "You feel angry and frustrated."
Client "Yes I do, I guess I just can't cope with all the hurt and upset of what is happening. I feel so guilty at times."

Reframing

This involves reinterpreting what is actually said by the client (which may in itself be a defence mechanism) into a more meaningful and valid understanding of their difficulties:

Counsellor "It sounds as though you don't really want to hit your wife. You want to hit her problem. After all, it is the problem that has virtually destroyed your relationship. Understandably you can't get at the problem directly, so you project your feelings onto your wife."

Reframing is a very useful means of addressing the real issues that are causing difficulties.

Confronting

Confronting the client directly, either with their feelings, their actions/inactions or even with an idea the counsellor may have, challenges them into action:

Counsellor "You feel angry because your wife can't comfort you or appreciate your efforts. Maybe you need to look at ways in which you can comfort yourself?"

In this example the counsellor is challenging the client directly to confront the impact his wife's difficulties are having upon him. If the client is to develop as a result of this challenge he must begin to change his actions, from attempting to make his wife change in order to meet his own needs, towards looking at ways in which he could nurture himself.

At times the clients themselves may challenge the counsellor to collude with their feelings or actions:

Client "He just kept on and on asking me the same question day in and day out. I couldn't take it any more, so I put a whole load of tablets in his tea — you must think I'm a real bastard."

Rather than colluding with the client, a more appropriate response might be:

Counsellor "I can see it must have been very difficult for you. People often act in ways which are against their better judgement when under severe stress."

To summarise, the objectives of counselling are to encourage the client to understand the circumstances of their difficulties; to help them to explore and express their feelings openly; and to help them work through overcoming their problems through action. The approach is developed in an atmosphere of trust, unconditional acceptance and positive self-worth.

The methods used involve attending and listening, open versus closed questioning, reflection, reframing and confrontation. Humanistic theory underlies the processes of awareness and change.

Problems in Counselling

Transference and counter-transference

Inevitably, in any close therapeutic relationship, feelings of trust and warmth develop between client and support worker. Indeed such feelings are important if the relationship is to progress effectively. However, for many reasons, there are times when the feelings that a client develops towards the support worker, or vice versa, can exceed the normal boundaries appropriate to that relationship.

The assumption is that the unmet needs, feelings of anger or love towards others which cannot be adequately expressed are 'transferred' by the client to the support worker or 'counter-transferred' by the support worker towards the client. In some forms of psychotherapy, transference is encouraged, but using the transference effectively requires formal training and supervision. Attempting to work through transference without formal training or supervision can, at the very least, place the relationship at great risk.

Identifying if and when transference begins to occur is therefore important. From the client's perspective, signals of transference include: the frequent re-emergence of the difficulties or issues which, they might have thought, were already worked through in the past; excessive anger or upset at the suggestion of terminating the relationship; being blamed or credited for changes for which you have no obvious responsibility; striking changes in the client's presentation or behaviour as compared with the previous sessions.

From the counsellor's perspective, signals include: a tendency to want to continue the relationship in the absence of any identifiable need; extending the normal boundaries of time and contact etc; experiencing excessive positive or negative feelings towards the client.

Should transference be identified as becoming a major issue in counselling it is strongly advised that you seek supervision or discussion with a relevant professional. As a general rule: (a) be honest with yourself and your client if you feel transference is taking place; (b) never devalue either your client or yourself because of its existence, rather work towards understanding; and (c) always direct effort towards arriving at an agreed and acceptable course of action.

Termination difficulties

Whilst transference itself can prove a major hurdle in successful termination, problems of disattachment can be equally difficult. It is likely that the relationship has seen major changes in the client and has proved to be a primary source of support and security for them. As a result, attachments, to a greater or lesser extent, are inevitable.

Although the clients may have reached a stage in their own development where they feel strong enough to cope, again it is worth while seeking advice if you feel the problem cannot be dealt with in the confines of the relationship. If necessary, refer the client to a specialist bereavement counselling service. In any event, the issue needs to be raised and is often dealt with as a formal pre-bereavement issue.

Taking the world on your shoulders

Very often, a client may express a vast array of difficulties which compound their presenting problems. It is important from the outset that you clarify what issues you are prepared to work on with your client and which difficulties may need additional help. It is very easy to continue a relationship indefinitely and by doing so exceed your own responsibilities.

Dealing with disclosures of criminal acts

From time to time, relatives may disclose in confidence that they have committed some form of criminal act towards their dependant. This is always a very difficult situation to deal with and should be taken seriously, especially if the actions of the relative are continuing. Inevitably, such information compromises the boundaries of confidentiality.

Should you feel that the nature of the disclosures abrogates normal discretion (given that the nature of relatives' support work is likely to yield difficult circumstances) it is advisable to seek the advice of a third party, such as a social worker or medical officer, without disclosing the names of the client involved, prior to taking any form of formal action. There *are* times when formal action is necessary.

INTERPERSONAL PROBLEM COUNSELLING

A client may often present with severe emotional conflicts due to being 'stuck' between two opposing courses of action, leading to indecision stress, such as whether or not to release their relative to institutional care. Alternatively, they may be experiencing feelings of guilt or self-reproach as a consequence of acting in a particular way towards their relative (eg. abuse) or going against certain promises or expectations to which they committed themselves prior to their relative developing their confusional disorder (eg. having an affair).

In either situation, providing an environment of acceptance is a major objective. It is important to follow this up by helping the client explore the positive aspects of their actions or feelings through reframing and confrontation. The client may indirectly be looking to the support worker for some form of 'licence' to justify their actions, but it is important that the support worker helps the client to achieve this 'licence' themselves. For example, in the case where the client is undecided as to whether or not to release their relative to professional care, the quality of the existing relationship between the relative and their dependant needs to be highlighted, in that continuing to care for the dependant at home leads to prolonged stress. However the time the relative has for themselves while their dependant is being cared for can be a time when the relative is able to readdress their own needs, so that they can invest more time and effort when they are visiting their dependant.

Alternatively, in cases where the relative may have met their needs outside the existing relationship, it is important that they explore the extent to which their own needs can realistically be met within the existing relationship. Either way, the client is likely to require a great deal of support in working through their difficulties and arriving at an acceptable conclusion which does not burden them with feelings of self-reproach.

BEREAVEMENT COUNSELLING

Caring and living with a confused dependant involves a prolonged bereavement process. In addition to the loss of the dependant's personality and the quality of the relationship the relative once had with the dependant, there is also the grief sustained when the relative needs to release their dependant into institutional care. Very often a client's presenting difficulties can in fact obscure a continuous bereavement reaction and it is important that the support worker recognise that this may be the case and confront the client accordingly.

While the experience of grief varies among individuals, there are four levels or stages which can be roughly identified:

1 Accepting the reality of the loss;
2 Grieving at the loss;
3 Adapting to new roles;
4 Reinvestment of emotional energy towards formulating new relationships.

Accepting the Reality of the Loss

Whilst the client may report that they have understood and accepted that their dependant has a confusion-related disorder and may be able to describe what has been lost in terms of their dependant's personality, intellectual functioning, dignity and quality of relationship, they may not have accepted the loss at an emotional level. Indeed they are likely to be very busy attempting to distract themselves from feeling grief through their daily routine.

If the client's report of these losses is rather matter-of-fact, or they reveal an inaccurate understanding of their dependant's difficulties ("Well, it's not likely to get any worse is it?") then these are clear indications that the client has not accepted at an emotional level what has happened. In addition, they may continue to behave as if there was nothing wrong with their dependant at all.

Grieving at the Loss

The open expression of emotion as a means of addressing the emotional consequences of loss is a very important process in bereavement. If this process is inhibited in some way, the client is likely to 'act out' their grief in a number of ways, such as spontaneous anger, euphoria or withdrawal. Indeed the stress that occurs as a consequence of withholding grief can often lead to physical ailments, such as chronic fatigue, frequent colds and hypertension.

Adapting to New Roles

As the dependant gradually loses their abilities to accomplish the tasks and activities which they could do prior to their disorder, so the demand for the relative to engage in these activities increases. Often, within this age group, sex-role stereotyping is much more clearly defined. Indeed many tasks — cooking, paying the bills, upkeep of the home, servicing of the car and so on — were tasks specifically undertaken by one party (particularly in the case of spouses). Therefore, if the relative is to maintain these activities, it is likely that they will need re-education and support.

Reinvesting Emotional Energy in New Relationships

This stage is perhaps the most difficult for the relative to address and is particularly pertinent to marital or common law relationships. It is very difficult for the relative, even though they may have accepted their emotional needs, to develop relationships with others without a sense of corrupting the promises, expectations or memory of what they had once had with their dependants. This is compounded in cases where the relative has strong religious views.

In stage 1 the role of counsellor is directing the client towards describing the events and experiences surrounding the initial loss. Stage 2 involves encouraging the client to make an open display (either with the counsellor or in private) of their feelings towards the loss. This may involve the use of reminiscence, old photographs and/or bringing to the session such symbols as reflected the personality of their loved one (eg. an article of clothing or something that the person has made). It is particularly important that an environment facilitating warmth and empathy is developed, since the open expression of feelings in this way can often lead to immense feelings of vulnerability in the client. As a general rule, the role of the counsellor here is providing the clients with a 'permission' to feel.

The third level can simply involve advice or education aimed at helping the client to accomplish certain tasks. If it is beyond the ability of the support worker to provide this, it is important that they have access to other sources of information or individuals who can provide support at this stage. Finally, with respect to the final stage, the role of the support worker is to help the client explore their needs and work through resistances by using reframing and confrontation.

STRESS MANAGEMENT AND COUNSELLING

Stress is an inevitable part of caring for and living with a confused dependant. Stress management is therefore aimed at stress control, not stress reduction. While it is impossible completely to eradicate stress from such a relationship, it is possible to address both the problems that give rise to stress and the way in which one copes with the consequences of stress more effectively. Stress management, therefore, involves two areas: self-management, and problem management.

Self-management involves structuring the daily routine in a way which provides periods for the client to develop some form of relaxation activity and to increase the degree of social involvement they engage in with others; helping the client to reframe their attitudes and thoughts when involved in stressful situations; and exploring ways in which they can obtain periods of restful sleep. In addition, it is important to encourage the client to enlist the support of others where practical help is needed — home help, respite care, bath nurse and so on.

With respect to problem management, that is, dealing more effectively with the specific difficulties that give rise to stress, the methods suggested in *Chapter 2* may prove useful.

WORKING WITH FAMILIES

Whilst the bulk of the support worker's role may be directed towards individual relatives, there are times when the 'client' is extended to incorporate the dependant themselves and/or the relative's extended family. Family work is in itself both a sensitive and a highly-skilled area and it is advisable that the support worker has some knowledge of family dynamics. The difficulties that families experience cluster around three main areas:

1 The practical difficulties encountered in adapting to new demands created as a result of caring for the dependant.

2 The difficulties encountered in adapting to changes in the quality of the relationship (emotional).

3 The influence of secondary gain in maintaining the family's difficulties and dynamics.

With respect to the first area, the difficulties encountered here result from changes in a family member's role, coping with the dependant's problem behaviour and developing a whole set of skills aimed directly at supporting the dependant's nursing needs.

The second area involves issues surrounding changes in the physical and sexual aspects of the relationship (the nature of which may in fact demand professional counselling), social issues (eg. being unable any longer to take part in social or recreational activities with friends), symbolic issues (eg. being unable to engage in personal activities which were once crucial in reinforcing the relationship — going to a cinema together or going out for a meal and so on), and finally issues surrounding love.

With respect to the notion of secondary gain (third area), this literally means the extent to which the consequences of caring for a dependant affect the way in which a family interacts. For example, the dependant may be a parent who is now living with their adult child who themselves have their own children living in the same house. The consequences of having a dependant living in these circumstances may be to offer a mechanism for keeping the children at home in order that they can support their parents' caring for their grandparent. Without this situation, the natural course of events might have meant that the children would find alternative accommodation elsewhere, so causing distress to their parents. Whilst this may cause frustration and anguish for the children, it means that the parents do not have to address their own separation anxieties. Consequently, the dependant may be being 'used' inadvertently to preserve the family's togetherness.

Obviously all areas call for a variety of approaches to be employed by the support worker in order to help the family work through their own particular difficulties. Further, the issue as to whether or not the dependant person is brought into the counselling relationship needs to be discussed, since, while they might be seen to be integral to the family system, their contribution may be limited.

Again, the objectives of working with families would be to help guide the family towards finding their own solutions and, where necessary, to support them in seeking the support of other parties.

4

Developing Support Services

SETTING UP A SERVICE

Before deciding how best to develop a support service for relatives it is advisable that three issues are given consideration:

1 That you have a clear understanding of the problems that relatives face and their specific needs for support at a local level. Communities differ racially, culturally, socially and economically, and each of these aspects has particular ramifications in providing support.

2 What facilities already exist in the area which can be co-ordinated to provide a range of support options?

3 What else might be required and how could one go about achieving this?

Much of this information can be readily supplied by voluntary networks and organisations, by prominent community members, general practitioners, community care workers and so on. Do also contact district health and social services departments who may be able to provide a list of relevant agencies, contacts, services etc and may even have involvement with local research projects.

Once in possession of these data, the next step would be to define the objectives of the service. What specifically are you trying to achieve? Who is the client and what is on offer? What boundaries will operate in terms of your role? In addition, the practicalities of the service need to be addressed. Is the service going to be localised and, if so, where? Are there going to be transport implications? Will the confused relative be involved or will they need to be supervised during counselling and support sessions? Who will be responsible for running and managing the service? Will other parties be involved? How will the service operate in terms of time? Will it be flexible in terms of responding to changing needs? Will you require any back-up support and, if so, who will you contact first?

In setting up a service, such questions will need to be addressed in order that it can run effectively and smoothly.

INDIVIDUAL VERSUS GROUP WORK

Support services to relatives can be delivered either on an individual basis, where the 'client' is a single relative or family unit, or on a group basis, where the client is the group membership.

With group work it is important, first, that the group membership is restricted to around six to eight people. Second, that the group members have very similar difficulties in common. Third, that group sessions are carried out at roughly the same time and in the same setting. Fourth, it might be advisable to undergo some form of pre-group assessment in order to clarify the specific nature of difficulties that the group are experiencing and to discern whether or not there are individual needs which may have to be addressed within the group context. Finally, a decision would need to be taken as to whether or not the group is essentially 'self-governing', in that the onus of support and change is placed upon the group members, or whether the support worker takes a more directive and personal role.

The principal advantages of a group are firstly that the group context is a powerful means for 'normalising' group members' difficulties: in one-to-one work the client can often feel alone with their difficulties, whereas in the group situation it is clear to each group member that other people suffer the same types of difficulties; therefore the individual does not see himself as being isolated. The group context is also able to offer a range of support and ideas that cannot be achieved on a one-to-one basis alone. Finally, the group may be able to facilitate its own self-help function in that group members may wish to contact each other outside the confines of the group session.

The difficulty with group work is that it assumes clients are able to interact freely. This is not always the case and some members may need far more support and guidance in doing so than others. In addition, individuals may find it extremely difficult to disclose very personal issues to other members, whereas in one-to-one situations they might find the development of trust far easier.

With one-to-one work, the approach is essentially client-centred and the individual is able to progress through support and counselling at their own rate and may in addition be able to work through particularly personal issues effectively. Individual work also has the additional benefit of securing the confidentiality of the client, whereas in group situations this cannot be assured.

Ideally, it would be beneficial if a support service could offer both one-to-one and group work, although from a practical viewpoint this is not always possible. In deciding which option to choose, one needs to consider the relative's needs, the objectives of the service, the resource implications in terms of time and manpower, and, finally, what other support services might be available.

ISSUES IN ACCEPTING SUPPORT

While it is recognised that relatives require support, this does not necessarily mean that they are able to accept what may be on offer. It is not advisable that one should think of the relative as a malnourished individual, ready and willing to be fed. There are several important and sensitive concerns which need to be addressed with the relative before they are exposed to any form of support service.

Time Constraints

Relatives are likely to be involved in some way or another with their dependant 24 hours a day. They are unlikely therefore to be able to take time out in order to obtain support themselves. This is especially difficult in the evenings when statutory (eg. day care) services are unavailable.

Feelings of Guilt

Relatives might feel extremely guilty at the thought of taking something for themselves when they could be devoting their energy towards their dependant. They may feel that accepting support is a sign of failure — of broken promises. In addition, they may ask themselves whether or not they are able to open up to another person and disclose very sensitive and possibly embarrassing issues.

Supervision

Many relatives, understandably, would be very cautious about accepting someone who is to look after their dependant when they attend support groups. They may question whether or not that individual could be trusted to look after the dependant, especially should a crisis occur. The success or failure of a support service can often rest solely on this one factor.

The Health of the Relative

Very often, the relative is a frail elderly person who might just be able to meet the daily demands of shopping, cleaning and so on without the additional investment of energy necessary to attend support meetings. In these cases it will be advisable for domiciliary support to be made available to the relative.

The Consequences of Support

Relatives may ultimately believe that, whatever support or advice is on offer, nothing will really change: the pressures and difficulties they undergo are an inevitability of their circumstances. In some cases, the relative may even be frightened that receiving support and counselling may change the nature of the relationship they have with their dependant.

Trust

Finally, many relatives will have unfortunately suffered severe setbacks in previous attempts at gaining help. They are likely, therefore, to show scepticism and hesitation when help is again on offer. It is important that every attempt be made to clarify the nature of the support which is on offer and that the relative is by no means compelled to accept it.

SUPPORTING THE SUPPORT WORKER

Supporting relatives in a structured way can be a very rewarding experience. It can also have its difficult and emotionally taxing moments which, if left to continue unabated, can lead to 'burn-out'.

Burn-out is a widely accepted phenomenon characterised by a number of features, which include: an inability to sustain attention on the task; gradual avoidance of working demands; feelings of depersonalisation; difficulty in understanding and solving even simple problems; and acute stress reactions (eg. spontaneous crying, extreme fatigue).

A major factor in precipitating burn-out is literally doing too much of the same thing too often. In part, this can occur because people may not be very accomplished at time management: that is, they are unable to prioritise their commitments, allocate sufficient time to complete them, delegate responsibilities to others more able to complete the tasks or simply to say, "Sorry, I can't." Alternatively, an individual may not be accomplished at self-management — the ability to recognise stress and seek appropriate support.

In counselling relatives, one shares very emotive experiences with the client — experiences which can tap powerful emotions in the helper, especially if they have been through similar experiences in the past. Sharing such pain is an important part of the therapeutic process. Indeed, if you have gone through similar experiences, this can often lead to a deeper awareness of the client's needs. However, if such past experiences have left unresolved conflicts or unexplored emotions, this can compromise the therapeutic relationship.

A more difficult issue might be that the helper is undergoing some form of displacement, in that difficulties or unmet needs in their personal life have been nurtured by their work commitments. The greater the need, the more engrossed one can become in the helping relationship.

If burn-out, displacement or your own emotionality become an issue in the relationship it is vital that you seek support yourself and, if necessary, ask someone else to continue with the case. In any event, it is advisable that formal supervision is sought as a matter of course in such work.

Appendix I
Further Reading

COUNSELLING (GENERAL)

Brumfitt S, *Counselling,* Winslow Press, Bicester, 1986.

Egan G, *The Skilled Helper,* Brooks/Cole, Monterey, California, 1986.

Knight B, *Psychotherapy with Older Adults,* Sage, California, 1986.

COUNSELLING (SPECIFIC)

Burnham JB, *Family Therapy,* Tavistock, London, 1986.

Charlesworth EA, *Stress Management,* Corgi, London, 1987.

Worden JW, *Grief Counselling and Grief Therapy,* Tavistock, London, 1986.

CONFUSION AND MANAGEMENT

Gilleard CJ, *Living with Dementia,* Croom Helm, London, 1984.

Holden U, *Thinking It Through,* Winslow Press, Bicester, 1984.

Murphy E, *Dementia and Mental Illness in the Old,* Papermac, London, 1986.

Stokes G, Series on *Common Problems with the Elderly Confused,* Winslow Press, Bicester, 1986.

Wilson J, *Caring Together,* Kings Fund/National Extension College, 1988.

The Health Education Authority, *Who Cares?,* London.

SERVICES FOR CARERS

Richardson A, Unell J and Aston B, *A New Deal for Carers,* Kings Fund/Health Education Authority, 1989.

Appendix II
Professional Workers' Glossary and Voluntary Organisations

PROFESSIONAL WORKERS' GLOSSARY

Health Authority

Chiropodist Provides specialist advice and aids for foot care.

Clinical Psychologist Non-medical specialist involved in the assessment, treatment and management of cerebral, emotional and behavioural dysfunction.

Community Psychiatric Nurse Provides holistic psychiatric and nursing care for people with psychiatric/psychological difficulties in their home or community setting.

Continence Adviser Provides specialist advice and aids for the management of incontinence.

District Nurse/Health Visitor Provides specialist nursing care and health counselling in the client's home.

Geriatrician Consultant medical officer specialising in medical disorders in the elderly. Holds overall clinical responsibility for patients referred by the client's general practitioner.

Neurologist Consultant medical officer specialising in disorders of the nervous system. Conditions apply as above.

Occupational Therapist Specialist in the assessment and treatment or management of problems in basic self-help and daily living skills as a result of physical or mental ill health.

Physiotherapist Specialist in the assessment and treatment or management of mobility and related disorders including chronic pain resulting from muscle or bone diseases.

Psychiatrist/Psychogeriatrician Consultant medical officer specialising in disorders of mental health. Holds overall clinical responsibility for patients referred by the client's general practitioner.

Speech Therapist Specialist in the assessment and treatment or management of communication and related disorders.

Social Services

Home Help Provides support and practical help to relatives and dependants.

Social Worker Assesses the social care needs of the dependant and their relatives and arranges for the appropriate services to become involved. They also provide personal counselling and support in times of difficulty.

VOLUNTARY ORGANISATIONS

These are non-statutory agencies who are able to provide a variety of services from day and, in some cases, residential care to help with shopping, gardening, general support at times of emotional crisis, information, sitting services and so on.

The organisations listed below would be able to advise on the availability of local services.

Age Concern England
Bernard Sunley House
Pitcairn Road
Mitcham
Surrey CR4 3LL
081–640 5431

Age Concern Northern Ireland
6 Lower Crescent
Belfast BT7 1NR

Age Concern Scotland
54A Fountainbridge
Edinburgh EH3 9PT
031–225 5000

Age Concern Wales
1 Park Grove
Cardiff CF1 3BJ
0222 371821/566

Alzheimer's Disease Society
158/160 Balham High Road
London SW12 9BN
081–675 6557/8/9/0

Carers National Association
29 Chilworth Mews
London W2 3RG
071–724 7776

MIND
22 Harley Street
London W1N 2ED
071–637 0741